Redapples falling still

REDAPPLES FALLING STILL

For permissions and information on ordering books, contact operations@smallharborpublishing.com.

Cover art: Oormila Vijayakrishnan Prahlad, "Apple Lattice"
Editor: Jessie Truong
Publisher: Allison Blevins
Director: Kristiane Weeks-Rogers
Managing Editor: Bianca Dagostino

REDAPPLES FALLING STILL
SNEHA SUBRAMANIAN KANTA
ISBN 978-1-957248-70-7
Harbor Editions,
an imprint of Small Harbor Publishing
Special thanks to: The Wild & Precious Life Series and Kristin Vandeventer

Redapples falling still

Sneha Subramanian Kanta

Harbor Editions
Small Harbor Publishing

தந்தை மகற்காற்று நன்றி அவையத்து
முந்தி இருப்பச் செயல். (கூ௰எ)

— Thiruvalluvar

Contents

For Appa

Redapples falling still

Apples

Though I believe hunger, I believe more in fulfillment.
The sacred knot of a full stomach. Fistfuls of blue-

berries picked from a mountain, its silent spectacle.
The whole world being remade and going unnoticed.

A whole world can be contained inside a watermelon.
You bring me cut fruit from the kitchen and I know

this ritual by memory. First, sounds of your footsteps,
then cold water running over the still fruit. The precise

movement of your hands with the knife. The enunciation
of fruit against its sharp edge. Every piece falling

in different variables of sound, like plucking tea leaves,
or a rustling as when you walk through sugarcane fields.

On most days, I predict the fruit like a weathercaster will
forecast elements, which is to say there are permutations

in this exercise. In the year when I was away from home, in
a new country, I saw fruits hanging from most trees—

all autumn the redapples falling on a slope near the train station,
and everyone walking past its busyness. If you were

here, you would study the branches and tell me about the trees.
Then, when we would reach home, and I finish preparing

lunch, you would begin to wash the fruit to be eaten after
the meal. Then, fold your palms in praise to God, and sleep

under the wide incarnation of a sky in the yard. The redapples
falling still. The redapples falling still.

Psalm For My Father

Father of hunger :: who fed his brothers and sisters first
before eating, a morsel of puffed rice in his palm.

Father of night :: who calmed my blisters
when the roof in our government-quarters apartment
came crashing down on a soundless night.

Father of equal blood :: one-acquainted with seas
and the distance between them, like a cartographer.

Father of monsoon tides :: the rain has smaller hands
than a deluge. Who baptizes the child first?
Father holding water :: for my first thirst.

Father of divinity :: who asks for the names of beads on a japmala
like a silent temple gathering fog beside the still morning lake.

Father :: beside the funeral pyre of my mother
beside the funeral pyre of his mother
beside the funeral pyre of three brothers
beside the funeral pyre of his father
chanting the names of our dead near a river
making the soil under our feet holy.

Father of rivers :: praying to each
like they were his new-born daughter and grandmother.

Father of syntax :: unmoors the difference between malai and mala,
Father picking young coconut shells littered on the ground.

Father voice :: instils slumber as he speaks in Tamil
Father sings into a conch bell in praise of God
Father who learns many languages and dreams in one
Father who lifts his eyelashes like dawning in a country of strife.

Red

Father / Today I speak to you / in a language / akin to lightness / as though a row / of red butterflies / prance inside my belly / like an unborn child / You too / were born crying / & drinking from the ascendence of heaven / on earth / descending like a feather / from mauve sleets / of dawn / Your mother bled / like all mothers bleed / once the umbilical cord / is cut / You once said / your birth brought a flood / with needle-shaped raindrops / A birth is never liminal / but occupies all quarters / The smallest part of your brain / is where something holy / resides: / a combination of all childhood memory / fields of / rice / sugarcane / wheat / barley / cows & buffaloes tilling soil / the red light / of dawn / and tomato plants / lined like sisters braided together / When I say father / I see a young boy / scatter red seeds / into the brown soil / I see a bouquet / of tomatoes / strung like guitar chords / A crescendo / pushing over the surface / for birth / & utterance / for red / to scatter over fields / like diphthongs / preserved with symphony notes / for earth.

Mother Tongue | Father Tongue

You don't decipher Sindh in my surname.
        Not the vicissitudes
of migration through algae-green
        or sky-blue oceans.
Let me tell you a story in three parts—
        The first part
burgeons from my mother. The second
        from my father.
The last is sprouting from me. Listen.

My mother tongue is history.
        In Karachi, my nani is still
a young girl climbing wide rooftops
        while a British viceroy
partitions India – Pakistan
        using outdated maps.
Cartography turns into itself like plaits.
        A conch shell separated;
both parts holding the same oceanic sounds.
        In five weeks, a border
is drawn and a new map exiles families.
        A forced migration through
ships, where she watches the harbor being
        left— enters the smoky coast
of Bombay. Years later, on the brink
        of the Arabian Sea, meets nana.
Years later, I will say, "A love story to recount
        to my grandchildren".
At the touch of dawn, love enters our life
        like an omnipresent God.
Nana chants bhajans in Marathi, a hibiscus
        in his hand. Fisherfolk songs
on his tongue. The ocean from which nani
        arrives here is his sustenance.
The border between Sindh and Maharashtra

appears like an asterism.
We walk among the carpet of gulmohar
in elongated lanes
where women dream of weaving mogras
into ancestral realms.
My mother speaks in five languages
and dreams in three.
After her physical death, to the world
she will be a body.
In the depths of a forest I pass through
in another country,
she will still be the first word I utter
when languageless.
She says she would visit me as a bird
and I hear birds fly
in the first spring of a new year
under the escarpment.
There is no constriction after death.
She is still dreaming.

My father tongue is the silence of God.
As a boy, a schoolbag
on his shoulders, my father walks through
paddy fields of dawn mist.
He recites English alphabets and prays
in Tamil. When I close
my eyes, I hear him pouring puffed rice
into his siblings' plates.
Thatha and Patti are a steady river current
across all of Tamil Nadu.
Their last residence is near the Bhavani.
I will remember this river
as a place we go to pray for our dead.
My father is learning
the cartography of water travelling to another
shore. When he will first arrive
in Mumbai, it will be a day of torrential rain.
In an expanse of mountains,

my father remembers his childhood, the place
we run toward our entire lives.
As I pick young coconut shells slowly littering
the ground, he intently studies their
fragmentations. Every miracle is a design
in the shape of God. At night
we pray for our bones to hold onto life
while listening to rain.

My languages are inherited. Words
speckle like the yearnings
of a constellation rebirthing itself
through an arrangement
in the pyrocumulus where stars
burnish ridgelines remnant
from gloam. When my eyes open,
the first word is in English.

Broken Sonnet, Or I Want My Loved Ones To Be Alive

I left some of my softness by the flowing Bhavani River.
Years later, on an early June morning, you will move like
a saint to disperse [ ] there. I want my loved ones

to be alive like I want the last notes of musicality to linger.
Every time is auspicious when you become one as a body
of time fossilizes, sustains prehistoric years in an expanse,

the way our bodies constantly evolve under the blazing heat
of sunlight: here, the farmers are working their hands under
soil, your mother is adding a tempering to coconut chutney,

I am embroidering a shirt, and you are removing the tender
coconuts fallen on the ground as quietly as this afternoon
will pass. The entire night, bamboo creaks as winds pass.

You cover the feet of your father with a cotton bedsheet.
You tell me about water as the Bhavani runs, blue— so blue.

For my father, and his

வீரப்பன் சத்திரம்

for Thatha

After the evening completely set
but didn't disappear into fragm-
ents, we walked to the temple in
another lane. Idols as quiet as the
grief in your body. Roads here are
elongated, linear. Every step leads
to a house with kolams outside,
dawn drawn, after sprinkling water
on the soil, bangles mingling with
the coarsely ground rice powder.
Yesterday, we walked here, and
today, the path still here, scraping
clouds from the sky, its white, in
another country, as falling snowflakes.

Shared Ritual

In the dream,
the fields are green again,
the river is unnamed and runs like rivers
run, connecting with another artery of water, running into
the shore of another village. Against the light, we are
travellers carrying pails of water for our thirst.
Who passed before on this path, a friend
in the night, looking for water
looking for respite?

Like Glass

The evening passed like glass on a train from Frankfurt
turning cirrocumulus clouds into a sleet of molasses sky

emulsifications. A passenger on the train asked
for the title of a book in my hands—— a collection

of poems by Rilke with papers on which I translated words
in the poems into German. We exchanged notes for exact

meanings of words, of which the two I remember
are Schatten, Herbst. We passed a station with

orange lights, not unlike eventide when my father and I
were going to Kumbakonam. I cannot think about shadows

without the bluish orb of carrying a memory: night shadows half-
covering seats, our faces like an offering of river-water

before entering the temples. I heard an animal shrill across
the tracks, and looked at vast expanses in the city to locate
the decibel-source. My father began translating Thiruvalluvar

outside the train window, greening fields in full momentum
kept flowing like time. The granularity in the landscape was
held between our bodies like an echo. The evening like glass.

Exegesis

A daughter is a speculation and the night sky. When I first
learnt about extinction, I asked my mother for a fruit, to
be cut in halves. My mouth remembers the first thirst like

the core of an orange. For all that parches us, we dance,
streaks of bandaged movements across the woundless sky.
My father tells everyone: My daughter is wonderful. I grieve

but surrender to infinite parables about the meaning
of being alive. Every time we meet, my father brings apples.
I spend another year retracing memory from its seed.

Which part of remembrance is the bluest? It is summer.
We sit under a sprawling banyan tree on the outskirts
of सातारा and my grandmother speaks about सांझा चुल्हा.

The landscape of coarse-sand, sprawling-green, steel-plates,
highway ends. The diameter of remembrance. Shadows
of trees I embrace, leafing like river streams beneath the sky.

A daughter is memory and knowing. The flesh is static
against the roar of midday. I joke again about a minor
thing, and my father laughs the loudest. I want to record

his laughter for the cold days. The scent in our kitchen
is like bulbs of camomile kept on the counter overnight.
I want to create something fierce but tender, bluer than

the faintest memory. The symmetry of loss is like the sky,
an everchanging expanse. I seek not neutrality but solid
color. My first saree was a gift from my mother after I urged

her to bring me something to wear that I can wave in the
air and dance. I had finished my first major public dance
show. The saree was pink and with polka dots

green, yellow, orange, black, and brown. There are few
things that remain in memory as persistent as color.
A daughter is the wind and the lucidity of a wide blue sea.

Three Kurals For An Ancestor-Tree

1.

It begins with Pitru Paksha.
The veil between our ancestors
and this world is less.

With closed fists, we walk
toward a green tree.
I want no evidence of life.

A tree can become an embodiment of an ancestor.
The story begins this way. Our story begins this way.
The tree is turning into the shade

of turmeric in the landscape of rain.
A carotid shape Norway maple—
where its roots meet the earth, we offer food.

Thirukkural — 338 analogizes the body
and the soul like a bird
flying away, its eggshell left behind.

2.

Winter. The trees are full again
laden with snow. How our landscapes borrow heaviness

from the changing seasons.
Everything belongs to everything else.

Thirukkural — 496 alludes that even a majestic chariot
cannot tread a waterbody.
Neither can a boat roam the rims of land.

I have ceased being a wanderer.
There is no desire for the devotion
                    of a heart except the wide incantation of a sky.

3.

Thirukkural — 339 reflects death as being akin to sleep.
Where are you, then, asleep for centuries?
Sing to me the wisdom we may inherit

to step out of the Arjuna Chakra.
The only way out of the loops of birth and death
is to break oscillations of the wheel.

        How may my hands hold rain to embody the fullness
    of this world? How may the rain quench, like cloudburst,
any suffering? How may we become transcendental like rain?

Naganallur Rainstorm

When you return to a village where you grew up,
you belong to every village; the people are your own,
the citronella sky— these sunsets
have passed between us like an exchange
of fragmenting cirrocumulus
becoming the sky.

Yercaud

The day I return to a beloved poem
            reading aloud to my father

a shift in the refract of light and shadows
            brings morning rain.

The rain is torrential, like the distance
            between two countries.

Our voices oscillate between being
            monsoon clouds and rain.

I read four lines from Malaipadu Kadaam
            written in 210 CE.

These describe a litany of sounds
            heard in the hills.

Sugarcane nodes being broken,
            women husking millets,

communal songs, and farmers
            sounding drums to detract

wild boars from yam and turmeric.
            My father recounts the first

morning light peering
            through Yercaud Hills

when cycling toward a temple
            as a young boy.

A man says the Gods of plains
            are different from Gods

of ascended slopes in momentum.
The sky intermingles

a wide blanket of woollike
monsoon clouds.

When crepuscle enters
our bodies acclimatize

to being evanescing stars.
As the blurring rain

falls on our bodies,
we become echoes.

Poem In Which Everything Connects

for Mumma and Appa

I.

The ocean foam has a sound of its own.
At Rameshwaram, southerly winds

pilgrim upon silver strands of waves;
my father and I pick seashells

from the shore. My mother places each
shell on her ear. I am five

again, looking at her. It is May and
fistfuls of sunlight gravitate

into the ocean. The capillaries
of sound are vascular. She puts

two shells on both sides of my ear,
and history fossilizes into vibrations

of sundown-blue, its coarse-xanthophyll
texture on my skin. Today, the sky

II.

is pliable, under which we eat idlis
with coconut chutney, and puliyodharai.

In my family, after worship, ceremony
continues in food.

The conflux of sky fragmenting into fulcra
of purple-mound, copper-roof, cedar-brown

almost the color of புளியோதரை.
Our hands move through the ruins

of a harbor. We know water does not
separate but circumnavigates.

III.

The fractions of these skies affirm
we can be anything,

tethered to a mountain, sloping
immovable but flowing

equidistant from the light
like bioluminescence.

Every ritual begins with விருந்து
on a banana leaf.

IV.

My father has a repeated story
he likes to tell everyone— there is use

for every part of the banana tree,
a song I want to always hear

food on the வாழை இலை
food in our stomachs

assimilating morsel by morsel
like rain from cloudburst.

[in another language]

after Sappho

let it be known
the source and tributary are same

later, memory
lumps of burning hay

tell me what you know about leaving
somebody will

turn at the same road
beside school and garden

with their hand full of grains
with their hand full of grains

another nameless dusk
passing over the Arabian Sea

last rowboats
dimly visible

at the sealine hem
you, reading

from a holy book
syllables as crisp as the oncoming rain.

As Prayer

When I tell my father I'm preparing rasam,
he tells me the etymology of how the dish
came to be prepared in Tamil Nadu, a tale
he has inherited and passed onward. Like all
qualities he values most, this is about not
wasting any food, hunger, and inheritance.
We prepare sambar, the creation source
of which has many stories, including that
it was first cooked in Thanjavur in the 17th
century and the name source may stem from
in the Tamil word Champaaram which means
an assortment of spices. The masala is made
by drying various quantities of coriander
seeds, red chilli, tuvar dal, pepper, cumin
seeds, fenugreek seeds, and turmeric sticks
under the sun for four hours. Then, these
ingredients are ground to a smooth powder.
We begin by boiling tuvar dal until there
are no lumps, then bring an assortment
of vegetables. As a boy, my father brought
produce from the fields near his home.
Today, I have shallots, okra, carrots, and
beans. My father tells me to cut one potato
as it enhances the quality of sambar. When
I begin to squeeze the soaked tamarind pulp,
the stove is switched on and the oil begins
to sizzle. I add shallots, called சின்ன
வெங்காயம், which originated from
Southeast Asia, then travelled to India
and the Mediterranean. I add okra, also
called வெண்டைக்காய், first grown
along the Nile River in Abyssinia, now
Ethiopia. Carrots, first grown for its seeds
and leaves, domesticated in Central Asia

in 900 CE, which turned an orange tincture
after six centuries of being cultivated. At last,
the potato goes into this medley, first grown
in the Peruvian-Bolivian Andes between 8000
and 5000 BCE. In Tamil, carrot is மஞ்சள்
முள்ளங்கி and potato is உருளைக்கிழங்கு.
After the vegetables, I add the liquid pulp,
sambar powder, and salt. Then, the tuvar dal
and some water, until the vegetables are soft
but firm. I add some more sambar powder
mid-juncture. My father says when water floats
over the sambar, it is time to commence making
rasam. His mother and more mothers did not
want to waste the dal water, and created another
dish out of the remaining water, sometimes adding
tomatoes, or condiments such as pepper or red
chilies. Before the noonday sun rose above their
heads, in Erode, he witnessed farmers return
under the shade of a sprawling tree to eat food.
Every field had one or two accompanying trees,
and the steel box had sambar, rasam, saadam,
and a vegetable. After the sambar was relished,
rasam was the neutral-tone to set any weather
change aside. Then, curd was mixed with rice
at the end for cooling down the body. Memory
is like தயிர் சாதம் for how it stays in the body,
after the smallest part of our remembrance becomes
a holy remnant. My father and I have a trajectory
like the Kaveri River: being born as a spring from
near the hills, joining a bay, and in incessant motion.
Our conversations are like the story of how rasam
came to be an integral part of meals in a home,
like the hairpin bends before entering Wayanad,
a story before another story, like preludes to history.

Ceremonial

In my family, meals are a sacred, anticipated ritual. When I visit thatha in Erode, he tells me there will be relatives coming over. I do the expected thing— invite ten more families. For the feast without ceremony, I first gather ten bunches of spinach and eight bunches of dill from the fields.

In my notebook, I write: To purchase— Two kilograms of rice, one-kilogram chana dal, two kilograms of onions, one kilogram of tomatoes, ginger, and garlic. For powdered spices, I use the blend of turmeric, red chilli, coriander, and salt. For whole spices, I use tej patta and dalchini, cloves, and kali elaichi. I know the measurements from muscle memory. For our South Indian side of the family, I prepare two dishes from Sindhi cuisine. This is how the rivers meet each other, in our multi-generational family where we dream in four languages.

As I coarse-grind cadmium-green spinach and shamrock-green dill-leaves, my mother calls out to my grandfather to light the deepam as it is dusk. My father arrives and I give him a spoon to taste the first blend of Sai Bhaji. He helps caramelize the onions as brown as the plains around the Sutlej River.

In my family, everyone participates in the ceremony of making. My grandfather and father bend like lotuses in a pond when a bird passes overhead, touching the petals. I know I am closer to something holy. When the families come to eat, I lay out banana leaves. My father reiterates the same sacrament— we hold the holy prayer of nourishment in our hands.

You Once Told Me to Look at The Sea to Understand Life

As people who have moved all their life
movement lodges itself into our bodies
like a flower first turns to fruit, then ripe.

I sing by the horizon of mastless ships
disembodied; and here— ribbon of froth
carries a surplus of smoke into water.

After the effigy of fog, the burning world
brings us its last offer, but we know how
nothing is proportionate unless a lie.

Before creases of dead leaves sweep over
to the next town, another sun would have set.
We once travelled from coast to coast

until Rameshwaram. Even rain travels
back to assimilate into the same source, towards
a sea, where the rowboats still glisten

with torchlights held by those gone far.
I asked you the name for lost songs— and you
told me how the seabed thrums

and unfolds a blur of sounds in constancy.
Let us call the season winter, when even the sea
becomes translucent like snow.

For Sentimentality

It was long after that year when the remembrance ritual began. It came in somatic bursts, when I was walking, in the middle of work, chopping onions, or in the shower. The smallest part of my brain holds the memory intact: I can still feel as though I am outside the temple, inhaling the aroma of dewy jasmine strands. My mother gets a small portion out of the four-inch diameter to wear in her hair. My father knows I like champas, and always asks the flower-seller for one lone champa and hands it to me. He continues this love language ritual.

When I complete dance classes on summer evenings, my mother brings me home. On the way, we walk by streets speckled with parijatas, raat-ki-raani, Gulmohars with orange and red flowers and the evergreens. I remember her voice when she calls my father, slowly ironing out details that we will be home soon, asking when he will be back from the office.

On a June night when the south-westerly monsoon winds bring drizzles to Mahrashtra, my father asks if we must call my grandfather. I immediately agree. My father dials a number in the STD booth in a corner in Chembur, Mumbai, and my grandfather picks up the phone in Veerapanchatram, Erode. The familiar distance between longing and the night sky is wholly ours. Over three decades since, I realize I can slumber listening to my father speak in Tamil.

Sentimentality means you and I are elsewhere, or together, but we were together at one point in time in an exact dimension, and I honour the memory.

Dear Father,

While winter flees in the God sky with God eyes
I watch ruminations of earth over the escarpment—
a fleet of intercity buses. In the sky like a blue bowl
a plane creates a trail of tear over the edge of a forest
hills descending over the bright neon. The bridge
is the color of rust and birds flying overhead know
more than all of us. There are many synonyms
for home in multiple languages. You cover each inside
the pleats of a shawl and remove them one by one
in winter, each for a new day, a different yearning
at night, the border between two countries becomes

darker, almost invisible, looking like it was tied
in a pillory thread of lights, appearing to glisten
from above the skies. In my dream I'm moving
everyday towards the longitudinal tides of things.
At morning, I arrange two flowers on my table,
luminous at dawn. These countries may become dreams.

Because The Night Will Go On, You Say

and that won't be the end of light.
Today I taste syllables more trepid
than the distance between us.

When you tell me how the light
is scant at Marudhamalai
or how petrichor lingers

among the coconut trees,
I tell you it will be night soon,
by which I not only mean it will be night

but that I'm fearful for the world.
Sepia stars beckon arrival
for something larger than the sky.

A river slips and leaves greenness
on its banks. You tell me when a river
runs full, it compensates for the world.

The moon is stiller than the smallest flower
and you tell me how birds have begun
to look for shelter before the deluge,

how the pelecinid wasp does not sting,
and how every animal prepares
for an exodus while winds untether

blankets left to dry on clotheslines.
God made the world of water
and fruit for our hunger,

though the world often forgets,
and because the night will go on, you say,
dawn will be another opportunity to remember.

In-Bloom

after Sappho

The calculus of things:
petrichor   lungs of forests

We walk till the last post office of a country
                              though we know
the world is more   smithed

leafing   into alluvial   composites
linoleum hills   of emulsified sunlight
          vascular lake   first of spring

the fields ignite   like glass
   being made from liquid sand
மாங்கனி trees latticed over the skyline

          Bay Laurel trees burgeoning
rainlight stains   fossilized

the world is bioluminescence   carotene dusk
in inverse morning-blue   roots billowing

          with rainwater abridge
the outside lexicon of a heritage architecture

chlorophyll-green   continuing harbor
everyday, landscape   blots into history

                                        quickening
like water takes shape   backbone of tides

   winds erupt and lullaby   weaving gossamer
light   after the lightning,   cerulean-blue
artery of sky   streets awash with reflections
your hands carrying   holy syntaxes

a father is the earth revolving
light after the fog

Two Broken Sonnets

I.

When I eat rice with my hands days later,
I think of the paddy fields when passing Erode.
I prepare sambar the way you'd like it.
Something is always working for us,
I believe in things against time.
Autumn, and the already ripened gourds
stacked on supermarket shelves

not the fields where bulbs of turmeric
sprout on the far ends, not my hands touching
their porosity, not the glimmer of sunlit
patches visible from our wide terrace,
not your sound calling me
to be the lamplighter pouring gingelly oil
into inverted earthen mounds,

II.

not the countryless breeze
carrying syllable-wisps of my prayer.
Today, my throat is a different flower.
I imagine sounds of the swift gutter moving
through the city lanes

then, at gloaming, dawnbirds arrive again,
sit on electric wire poles as I bring a plate

of rice, you fill water, descending as I call
them, slowly, speckles of stars with wings,
before the skystars appear. The water motor
switched on, a rustling of coconut trees
your voice in this fleeting life, this fleeting

life which must stay longer than
moonlight silvering the Bhavani.

What Survives Us

When I went back to where we lived,
there I met history again, standing,
recalcitrant below the noonday sun.
The butterflies and the shops were gone,
the exterior of buildings in the colony
smelled of a fresh coat of paint.

Children were coming back from school,
not unlike me, turned younger now,
remembering the static occurrences—
time, defying gravity, landing
like a permanent thump. I unravel memory
not unlike a question of memory. Even today,

what wakes me is the prospect of dusk, the squared
windows still bringing breeze from the parijata trees.

Acknowledgments

My gratitude to the editors of these publications for first publishing earlier versions of these poems.

Apples :: MAZA Anthology 2023

Psalm for My Father :: Grain Magazine, Vol. 50.1, Fall 2022

Red :: Published in *Landscape* :: *Bodies*, winner of the 2018 Rhythm Divine Poetry Chapbook Contest

Broken Sonnet, Or I Want My Loved Ones To Be Alive :: Away From Home anthology, Stanchion, 2024

வீரப்பன் சத்திரம் :: Bodies A Preservation of Land & Self: A Poetry Anthology by Beaver Magazine, 2023

Shared Ritual :: Another Chicago Magazine, Online Issue, 2022

Exegesis, Ceremonial :: 128 Lit, Issue Two, 2023

Poem In Which Everything Connects :: Funicular 17, 2025

[in another language] :: Sundog Lit, Issue Twenty

You Once Told Me to Look at The Sea to Understand Life :: PRISM Magazine, 60.3 – MYTH, Spring 2022

For Sentimentality :: Astrolabe, 2023

Because The Night Will Go On, You Say :: ROOM Magazine, Tipping Point, 45.2, 2022

In-Bloom :: carte blanche, Issue 44, 2023

Two Broken Sonnets :: Gutter Magazine, No 29, 2024

What Survives Us :: Wet Grain, Issue 4, Summer 2023

Born in Mumbai, Sneha Subramanian Kanta is an award-winning writer, academician, and editor. She is the sixth Poet Laureate of Mississauga (2026 – 2028). She is the 2025 Woodhaven Artist in Residence at The University of British Columbia Okanagan, and the author of six chapbooks. Her work has been recognized and supported by Canada Council for the Arts, Ontario Arts Council, the Charles Wallace Trust, the Vijay Nambisan Foundation, and British Council. Her work has been widely anthologized internationally, including in The Penguin Book of Indian Poets (ed. Jeet Thayil). She is one of the founding editors at Parentheses Journal.

About Small Harbor Publishing

Small Harbor Publishing is a 501c3 nonprofit organization. Our goal is to publish unique and diverse voices. We are a feminist press, and we are committed to diversity and inclusion. We strive to bring new voices to a devoted and expanding readership.

Small Harbor Publishing began in 2018 with the first issue of *Harbor Review*. The magazine is an online space where poetry and art converse. *Harbor Review* quickly grew and now publishes reviews and runs multiple micro chapbook competitions, including the Washburn Prize and the Editor's Prize.

In July 2020, Small Harbor Publishing was officially incorporated and began Harbor Editions. Harbor Editions accepts submissions through a chapbook open reading period, a hybrid chapbook open reading period, the Marginalia Series, and the Laureate Prize.

In 2023, Harbor Anthologies began with a mission to promote texts that explore social justice issues and highlight marginalized writers.

If you would like to support Small Harbor Publishing, visit our "About" page at: smallharborpublishing.com/about.

www.ingramcontent.com/pod-product-compliance
Lightning Source LLC
LaVergne TN
LVHW051021080826
845145LV00009B/2741

* 9 7 8 1 9 5 7 2 4 8 7 0 7 *